Modules
by Paul Sheftel

INTRODUCTION

A module may be thought of as a unit or grouping. There is a great deal of "modularity" in modern times. Many of our electrical appliances, for instance, have modules or inner workings often located in a single unit which can easily be removed for repair or replacement. It is a useful concept when applied to learning, for it is always easier to learn things in categories or groups rather than taking each item separately. For example, when learning to play a C chord, why not also learn F and G chords, since they all use only white keys.

The three sections of modules are all about such groupings, concentrating on the 12 major scales, the perfect, major and minor intervals, and the 12 major triads in root position and first and second inversions. These are all studied in logical groupings. There is a specific musical composition for each scale, chord and interval.

The compositions have all been designed to be played either on pianos or electronic keyboards. No piece contains a span greater than four octaves. Players are invited to find appropriate sounds and rhythm backgrounds for each piece when using electronic keyboards.

Students are urged to work on the specific elements on which each piece is based: scales, intervals or chords, before working on the actual piece.

CONTENTS

ISBN 978-0-9824012-6-2
Library of Congress Control Number: 2009941407

YBK Publishers, Inc.
39 Crosby Street
New York, NY 10013

SECTION I
Major Scales: C, G, D, A, E (0 to 4 sharps)

Each new scale can be located by counting five notes up from the previous one. C, for instance, has no sharps. Counting up five notes from C (C-D-E-F-G) we get to the G scale with one sharp.

FINGERING

We can understand the fingering for any scale by knowing where the 4th finger is used, since it is used only once in any given octave, and always in the same place.

The fingerings for the C, G, D, A and E group of scales are as follows:

• Right hand: 4th finger on 7th scale step.

• Left hand: 4th finger on 2nd scale step.

KEYBOARD GEOGRAPHY

Seeing and understanding specific combinations of black and white keys can be enormously helpful in learning and remembering scales, chords and intervals. Study the following, carefully noticing how the sharps increase in symmetrical arrangements:

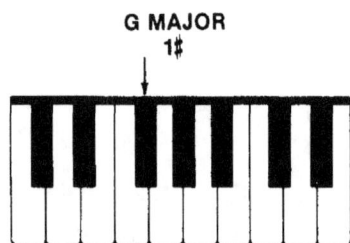

G MAJOR
1♯

(Bottom of 3 black-key group)

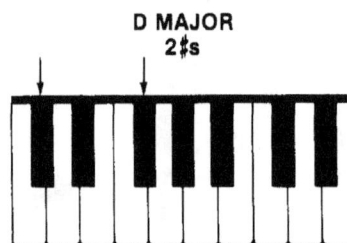

D MAJOR
2♯s

(Add bottom of 2 black-key group)

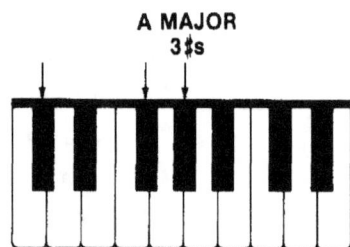

A MAJOR
3♯s

(Add middle of 3 black-key group)

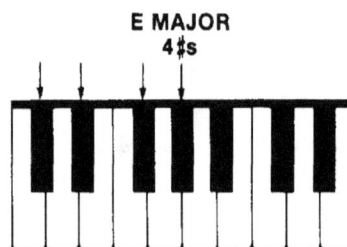

E MAJOR
4♯s

(Add top of 2 black-key group—2 + 2)

OBSERVATIONS AND ACTIVITIES

Correct scale fingering should be carefully observed when playing these pieces. Practice each scale before studying the piece based on that scale. Notice how the left hand accompaniments for the D, A and E scale pieces contain the black keys of the scale.

Scales: C Major

UPS AND DOWNS

PAUL SHEFTEL

ELEVATORS

PAUL SHEFTEL

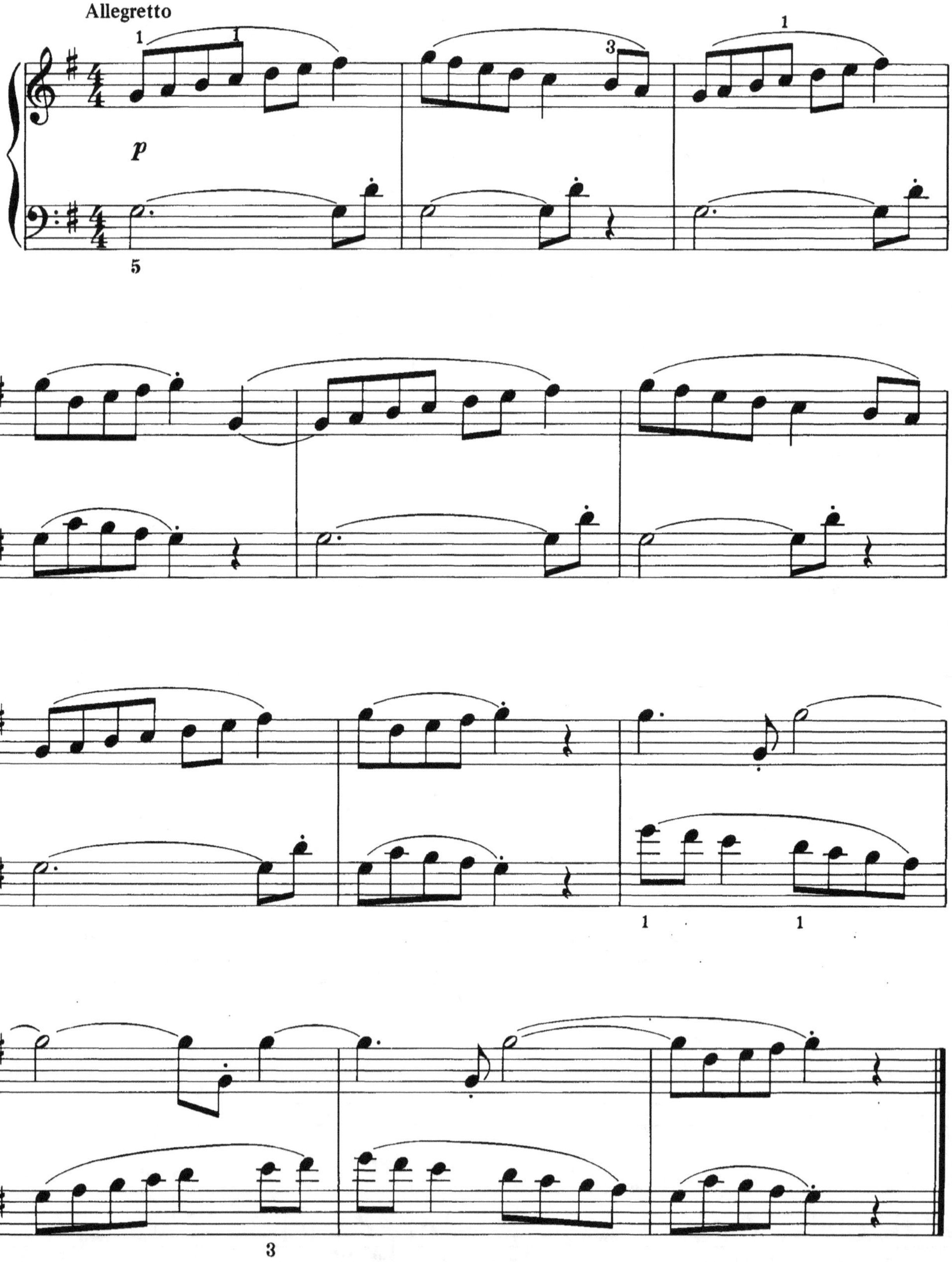

Scales: D Major

ASCENTS AND 'D'SCENTS

PAUL SHEFTEL

This piece sounds nice if you swing the rhythm of the eighth notes. Measure 2 for instance:

HIGHS AND LOWS

PAUL SHEFTEL

Scales: E Major

SEESAWS

PAUL SHEFTEL

Intervals: Perfect 4ths and 5ths

The distance between two notes is called an interval. The distance between the 1st and 4th scale steps is called a perfect 4th: between the 1st and 5th, a perfect 5th:

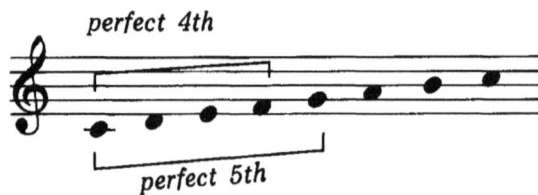

KEYBOARD GEOGRAPHY

PERFECT 4ths: white/white or black/black except when F and B are used (F-B♭, F♯-B). For example:

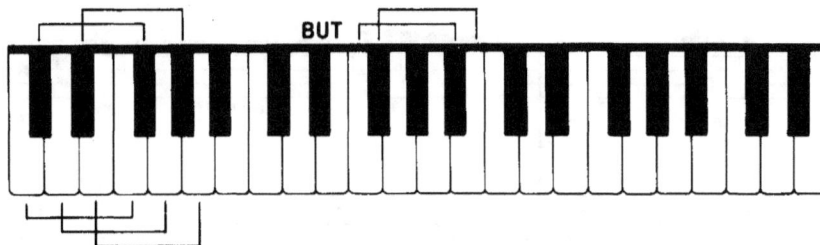

PERFECT 5ths: same as perfect 4ths—white/white or black/black except when B and F are used (B-F♯, B♭-F):

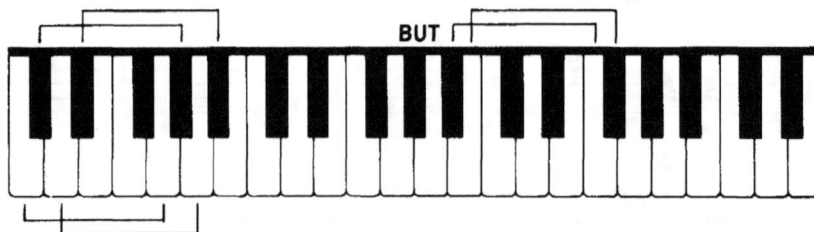

OBSERVATIONS AND ACTIVITIES

It will be noticed how each piece is built on the "keyboard geography" of the particular interval under study. Indicate with a check mark every interval which uses a combination of F/B♭ or F♯/B.

Practice playing 4ths and 5ths up and down the keyboard. Begin with those which use only white or only black keys.

Intervals: Perfect 4ths

FORTITUDE

Nicht zu schnell*

PAUL SHEFTEL

*German: not too fast. Why German? Well, it does add some variety.

A MIGHTY FIFTHFUL

PAUL SHEFTEL

Major Triads: 12 Keys Root Position

A major triad consists of the 1st, 3rd and 5th notes of a major scale. C major, for instance:

FINGERING:
1-3-5 in right hand; 5-3-1 in left hand.

KEYBOARD GEOGRAPHY
Major triads can be classified in three groups:

1. C, F and G: white keys only

2. A, D and E: (think of "lemonADE") one black key.

3. B: (think of "Killer B") two black keys.

The triads which have black key roots (start on black keys—D♭, E♭, G♭, A♭, B♭) fit this pattern in a mirrored form, each being the mirrored opposite of its upper white key neighbor. For instance:

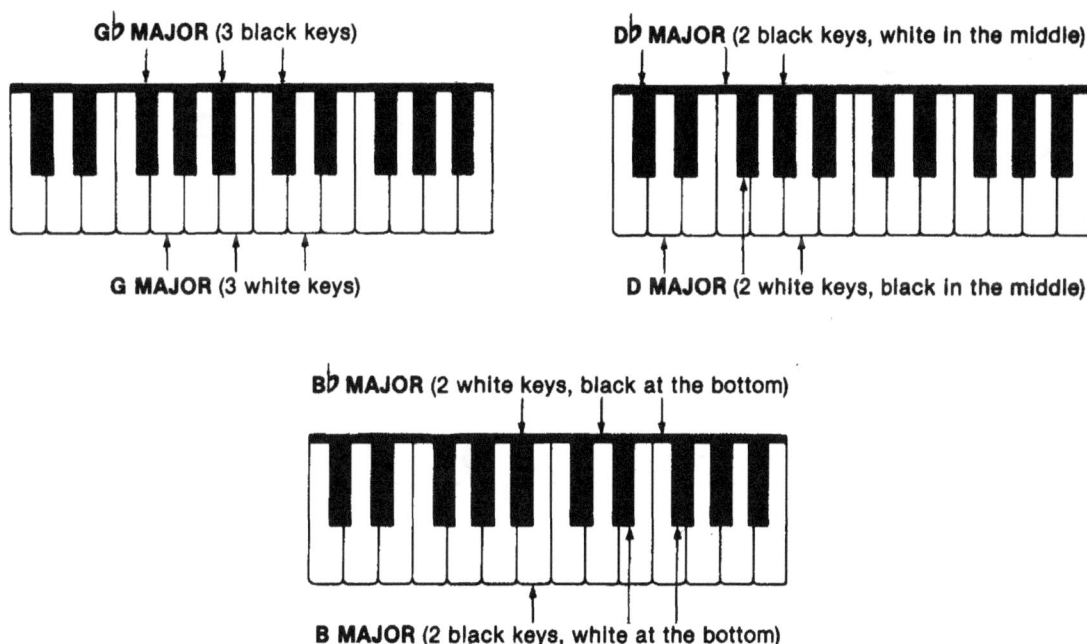

OBSERVATIONS
Five pieces explore the relationships of the following chords:
1. C, F and G
2. A, D and E
3. A/A♭, D/D♭ and E/E♭
4. B/B♭
5. G/G♭

Practice all these chord combinations before studying the pieces.

BOOGALOO IN C

Tempo di boogaloo

PAUL SHEFTEL

LEMONADE

With   quench

PAUL SHEFTEL

Triads (Root Position): A—D—E; Ab—Db—Eb Major

FANFARES

Majestically

PAUL SHEFTEL

TANGO

PAUL SHEFTEL

Sultry

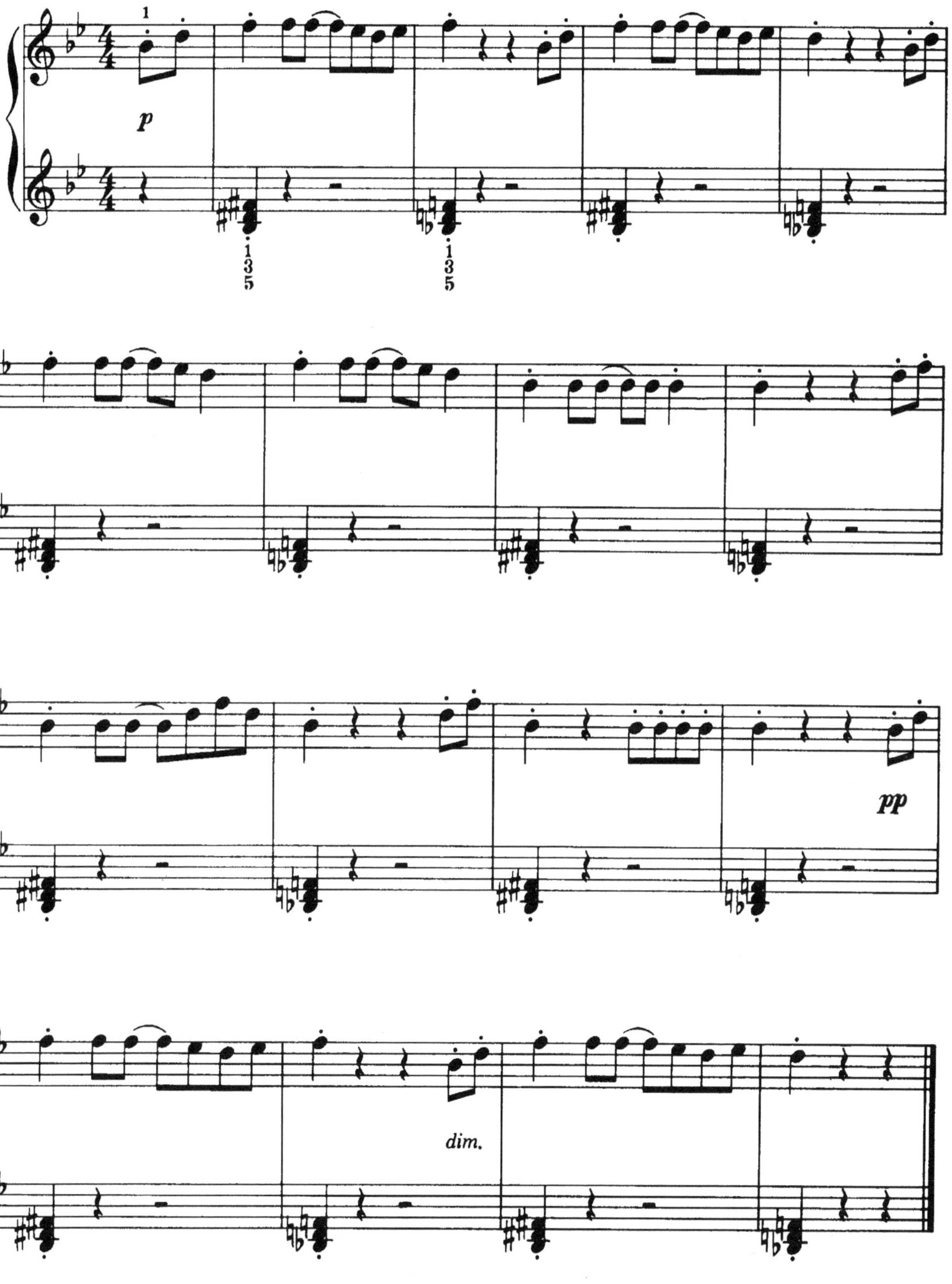

Triads (Root Position): G—G♭ Major

TANGLE

PAUL SHEFTEL

Lively

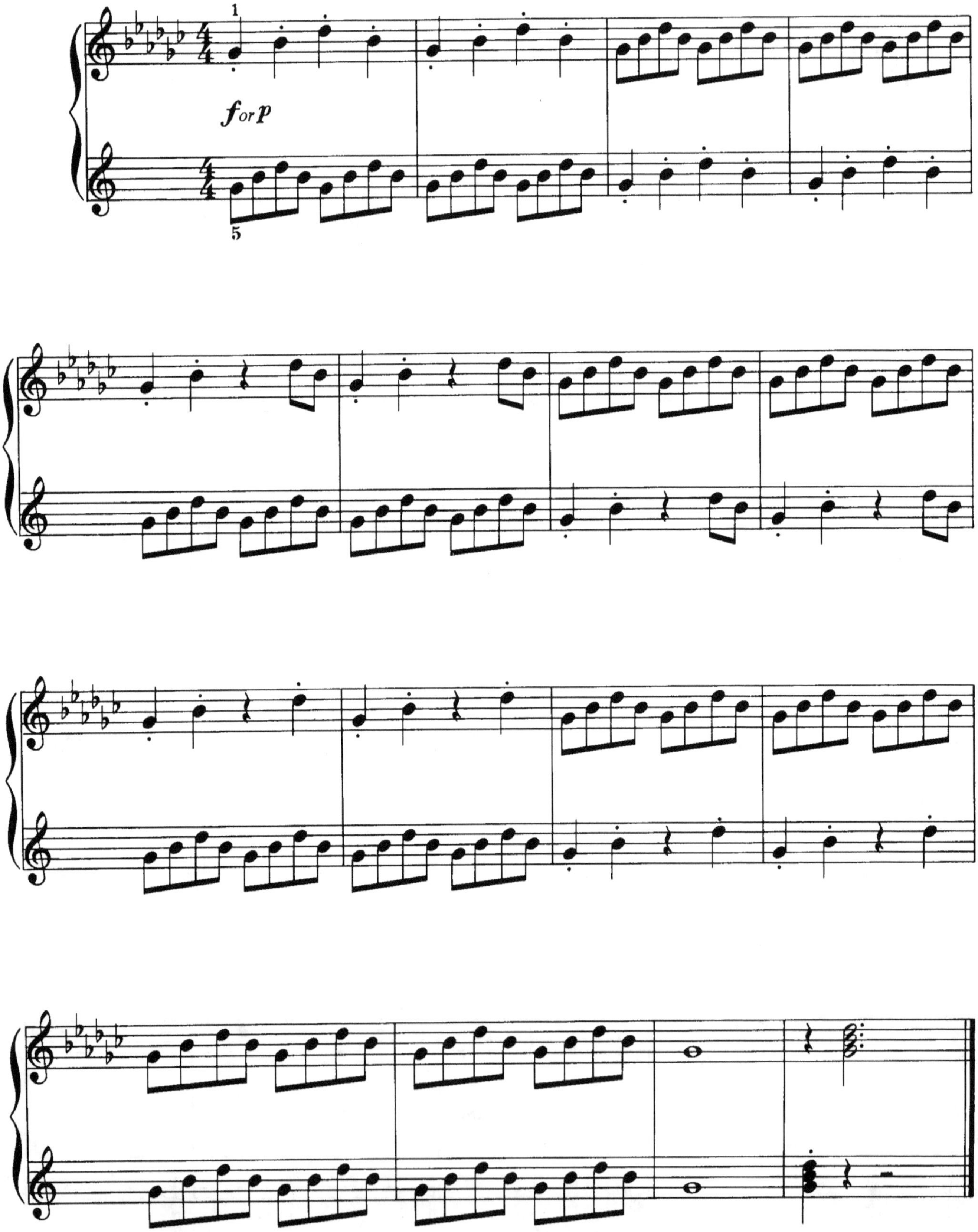

SECTION II

Major Scales: F, B♭, E♭, A♭ (1 to 4 flats)

Each new scale can be located by counting four notes up the scale from the keynote of the last. F, for instance, has one flat. Counting four notes up from F (F-G-A-B♭) we get to the keynote of the scale with two flats.

FINGERING
• Right hand: The 4th finger always falls on B♭ *and nowhere else*. EXCEPTION: when playing the F major scale you will also use your 4th finger at the end of the scale on F. On the B♭, E♭, and A♭ scales, however, your thumb will always be on F.

• Left hand: Start each scale with the 3rd finger. The 4th finger *always* falls on the 4th scale step. EXCEPTION: F is fingered like C major with the 4th finger on the 2nd scale step.

KEYBOARD GEOGRAPHY
Notice how the flats increase in a symmetrical arrangement mirroring that of the sharp scales:

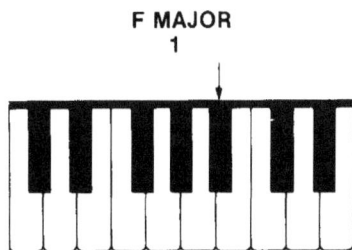

F MAJOR
1

(Top of 3 black-key group)

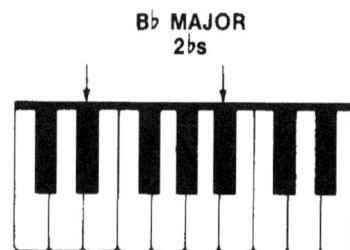

B♭ MAJOR
2♭s

(Add top of 2 black-key group)

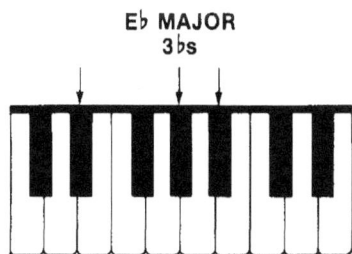

E♭ MAJOR
3♭s

(Add middle of 3 black-key group)

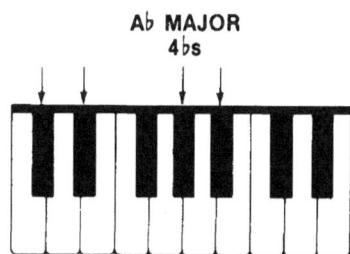

A♭ MAJOR
4♭s

(Add top of 2 black-key group—2 + 2)

OBSERVATIONS AND ACTIVITIES
Left hand accompaniments in the pieces all use black keys found in the scale.

Practice each scale before playing the pieces.

SECTION II

'F'FERVESCENCE

PAUL SHEFTEL

Bubbly but smooth

Scales: Bb Major

Bb BUBBLES

PAUL SHEFTEL

Scales: Eb Major

SONG

PAUL SHEFTEL

Scales: Ab Major

KANGAROO WALTZ

PAUL SHEFTEL

In the style of dancing kangaroos

Intervals: Major 2nds, 3rds, 6ths and 7ths

The distance from the first step of a major scale to the second is called a major second; to the third step, a major third; to the sixth, a major 6th, and to the 7th, a major 7th. Remember that 4ths and 5ths, as well as octaves, are called "perfect intervals." 2nds, 3rds, 6ths and 7ths (in a major scale) are called "major" intervals.

KEYBOARD GEOGRAPHY

MAJOR 2nds: white/white or black/black except in the "gaps" between the groups of black keys (E-F♯, E♭-F; B-C♯, B♭-C). For example:

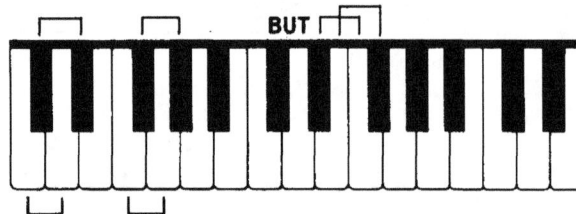

MAJOR 3rds: Just as triads starting on C, F and G, are all white, so are major thirds. Other than C, F and G, they are white/black starting on the white keys. All major 3rds starting on black keys are black/white except G flat, which is black/black.

MAJOR 6ths: One way to locate major 6ths easily is to play a perfect 5th and then enlarge it by a whole step (major second). There are two "clusters" in which each major 6th is one color:

Elsewhere, a major 6th is always either white/black or black/white.

MAJOR 7ths: These are particularly easy to locate on the keyboard. When built on a white key they are always white/black except for 7ths built on C and F which are white/white. Every major 7th built on a black key is black/white. (Another easy way to practice locating major 7ths is to play an octave and then reduce it by a half step.)

OBSERVATIONS AND ACTIVITIES

Each piece that follows is made up of musical patterns derived from the keyboard geography features described before.

Before studying the pieces, work at locating the intervals as described. Try improvising using different intervals.

Learn to recognize each interval by remembering tunes which start with that interval. For instance:

MAJOR 2nd

Frè - re   Jac - ques

MAJOR 3rd

Oh, when the   saints

PERFECT 4th

Here   comes the bride

PERFECT 5th

Twin - kle,   twin - kle

MAJOR 6th

My   Bon- ny lies   o - ver the   o - cean

Intervals: Major 2nd

SECONDS AWAY

PAUL SHEFTEL

Intervals: Major 3rds

TOCCATA IN THIRDS

PAUL SHEFTEL

THE SIXTH SHEIK'S SIXTH SHEEP'S SICK

PAUL SHEFTEL

Intervals: Major 7ths

IT'S HEAVEN UP HERE

PAUL SHEFTEL

Major Triads: 1st inversion

A major triad consists of a root, a 3rd and a 5th:

Triads in 1st inversion have the root on top, the 3rd on the bottom and the 5th in the middle:

The interval of a 4th separates the root from the note underneath.

FINGERING
All 1st inversion triads are played with 1-2-5 in the right hand, and 5-3-1 in the left hand.

KEYBOARD GEOGRAPHY
Major triads can be classified in three groups:

1. C, F and G: white keys only

2. A, D and E: (think of "lemonADE") one black key.

3. B: (think of "Killer B") two black keys.

The triads which have black key roots (start on black keys—D♭, E♭, G♭, A♭, B♭) fit this pattern in a mirrored form, each being the mirrored opposite of its upper white key neighbor. See *Keyboard Geography*, page 11.

ACTIVITIES
Point to any key randomly with either the 5th finger of your right hand or the thumb of your left, add a perfect 4th below. Then add the third note, the 3rd below the 4th, to complete the 1st inversion triad. Work through each of the chord groups. Example:

Pay careful attention to fingering.

OVER LIGHTLY

PAUL SHEFTEL

Lightly

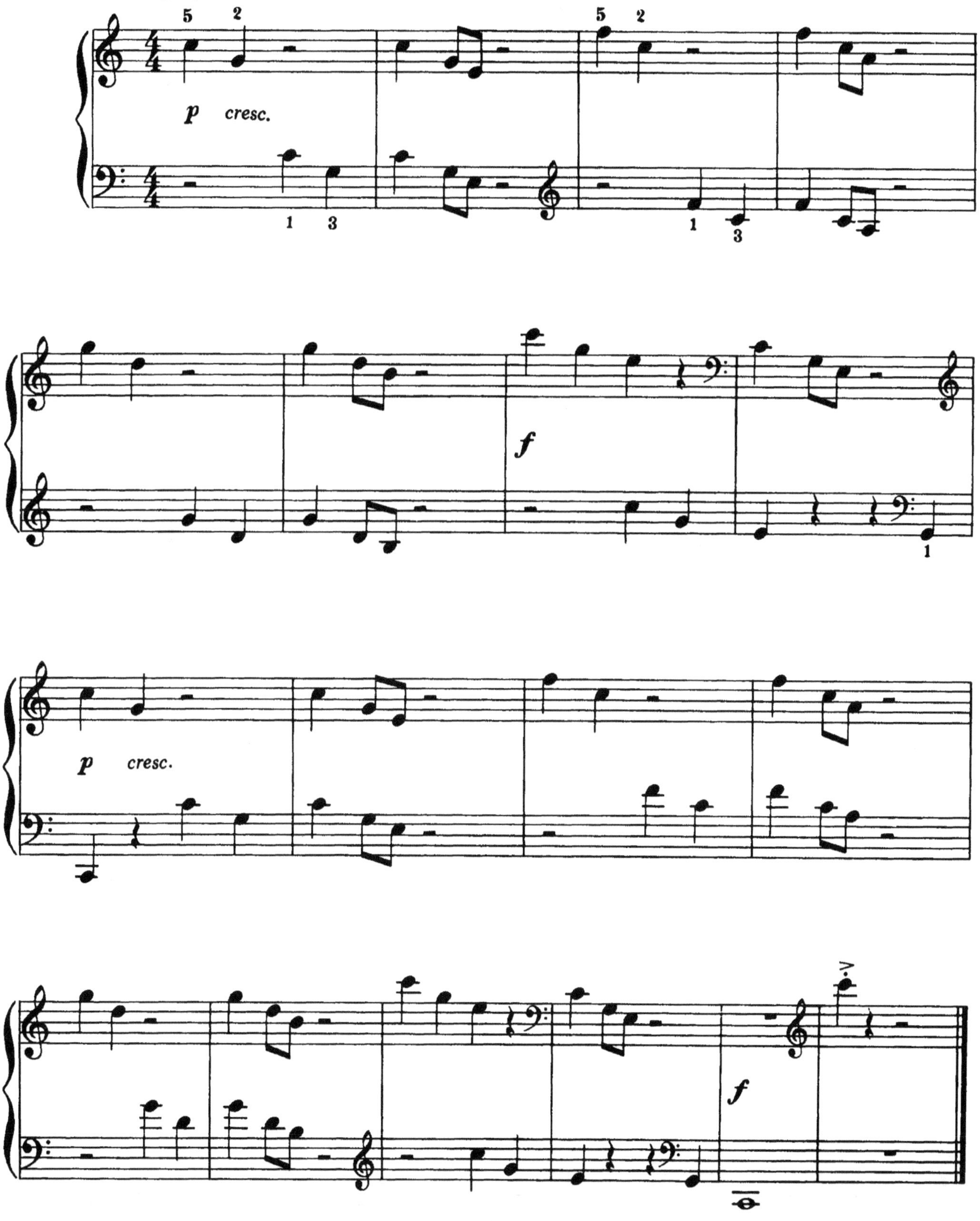

INVERSION DIVERSIONS

TARANTELLA

PAUL SHEFTEL

On the swift side

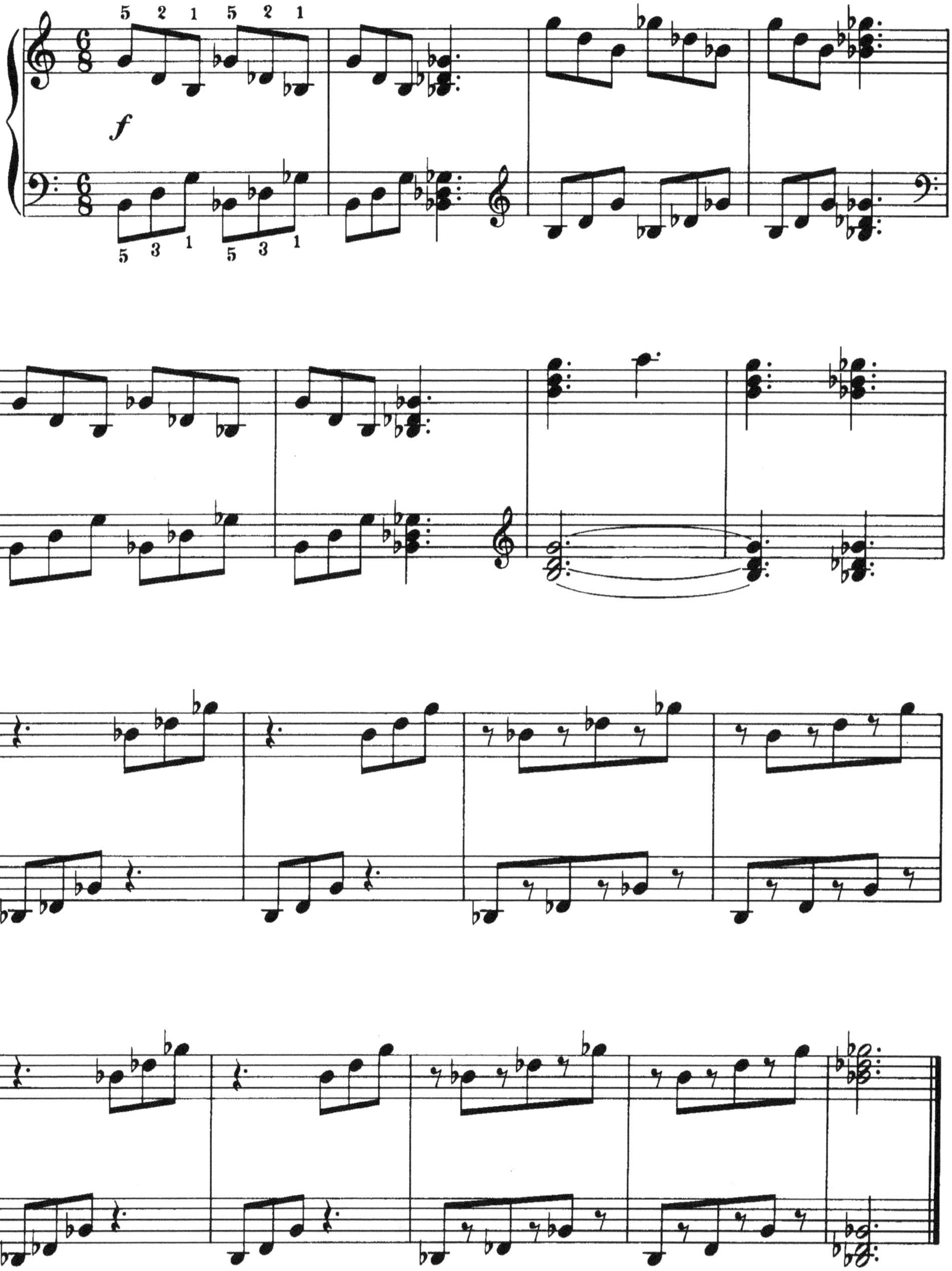

OLÉ

Lively

PAUL SHEFTEL

SECTION III

Major Scales: B (C♭), F♯ (G♭), C♯ (D♭) —(5 to 7 sharps or flats)

These scales have a number of things in common:

1. They are enharmonic—they can be considered either as flat or sharp scales (B/C♭, etc.). A point of interest: the combination of flats and sharps in the two enharmonic scales always adds up to 12. B, for instance, has five sharps; its enharmonic scale, C♭, has seven flats.

2. These scales all use five black keys.

3. They all use the same fingering: thumbs fall together on white keys; fingers 2-3 are used on the groups of two black keys, while 2-3-4 are used on the groups of three black keys.

KEYBOARD GEOGRAPHY—HOW TO REMEMBER WHICH WHITE KEYS ARE USED:
B (C♭): The lower of the white keys separating the black key groups are used.

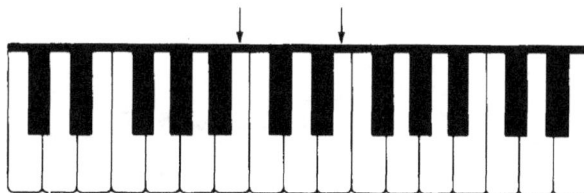

F♯ (G♭): The white keys on either side of the group of three black keys are used.

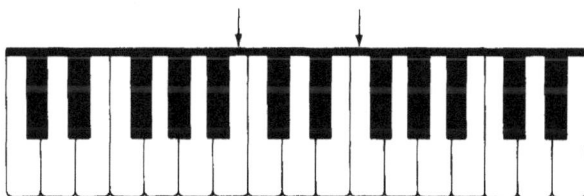

C♯ (D♭): The upper of the white keys separating the black key groups are used.

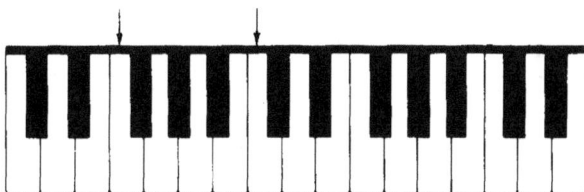

OBSERVATIONS AND ACTIVITIES
Practice each scale before playing the pieces.

SECTION III

NONE OF YOUR 'B'SNESS

PAUL SHEFTEL

Scales: F# Major

WINDOW SHARPING

PAUL SHEFTEL

Scales: C# Major

LOOK SHARP

PAUL SHEFTEL

Intervals: Minor 2nds, 3rds, 6ths, 7ths and Tritones.

Major intervals become minor intervals when they are *reduced* by a half step.

Major intervals and perfect intervals, when *enlarged* by a half step, become "augmented."

A "tritone" is an augmented 4th. It is called a tritone because it contains three whole steps, or major 2nds.

Augmented 4th:

Perfect intervals (4ths, 5ths), when made a half step smaller, become "diminished." A tritone can also be considered a diminished 5th:

Diminished 5th:

KEYBOARD GEOGRAPHY
MINOR 2nds: always white/black or black/white except in the gaps between the black key groups (E-F, B-C—white/white).

MINOR 3rds: white/black or black/white on C/C♯, F/F♯ and G/G♯; otherwise either white/white or black/black.

MINOR 6ths: easily located by playing a perfect 5th and then enlarging by a half step. The following formula can also be used: all white starting on E, A, B, otherwise white/black or black/white.

MINOR 7ths: These are particularly easy to remember—white/black or black/white on C/C♯ and F/F♯, otherwise either all white or all black.

TRITONES: always white/black or black/white except for the combination B to F or F to B.

OBSERVATIONS
This may seem like a great deal of information to learn and remember at one time. It is—so don't try! It is all very logical but take one step at a time. Work with one interval before going on to the next.

CLOSENESS

PAUL SHEFTEL

Intimately

Intervals: Minor 3rd

DEW DROPS

PAUL SHEFTEL

SHORT HOPS

PAUL SHEFTEL

Sort of like a baby kangaroo

Intervals: Minor 7th

LONG HAULS

Sort of like a baby dinosaur

PAUL SHEFTEL

Intervals: Tritone

A LITTLE STRANGE

PAUL SHEFTEL

Maybe a little like a baby brontosaurus

Major Triads: 2nd inversion

When a triad is in the 2nd inversion, the root is in the middle. The interval below the root is a perfect 4th.

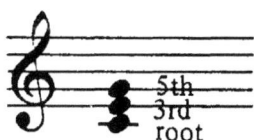

MAJOR TRIAD   **1st INVERSION**   **2nd INVERSION**

FINGERING

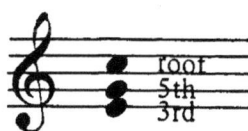

All 2nd inversion triads are played 1-3-5 in the right hand, and 5-2-1 in the left hand.

KEYBOARD GEOGRAPHY

Major triads can be classified in three groups:

1. C, F and G: white keys only

2. A, D and E: (think of "lemonADE") one black key.

3. B: (think of "Killer B") two black keys.

The triads which have black key roots (start on black keys) fit this pattern in a mirrored form, each being the mirrored opposite of its upper white key neighbor. See *Keyboard Geography*, page 11.

ACTIVITIES

Point to any key on the keyboard with the middle finger of your right hand or the index finger of your left. Play a perfect 4th below. Then add the third note, the third above the root, to complete the chord. Work through each of the chord groups. Example:

HYMN

Slowly, with feeling

PAUL SHEFTEL

*This chord is neither C, F, nor G major. (It's A minor.)

HOEDOWN

PAUL SHEFTEL

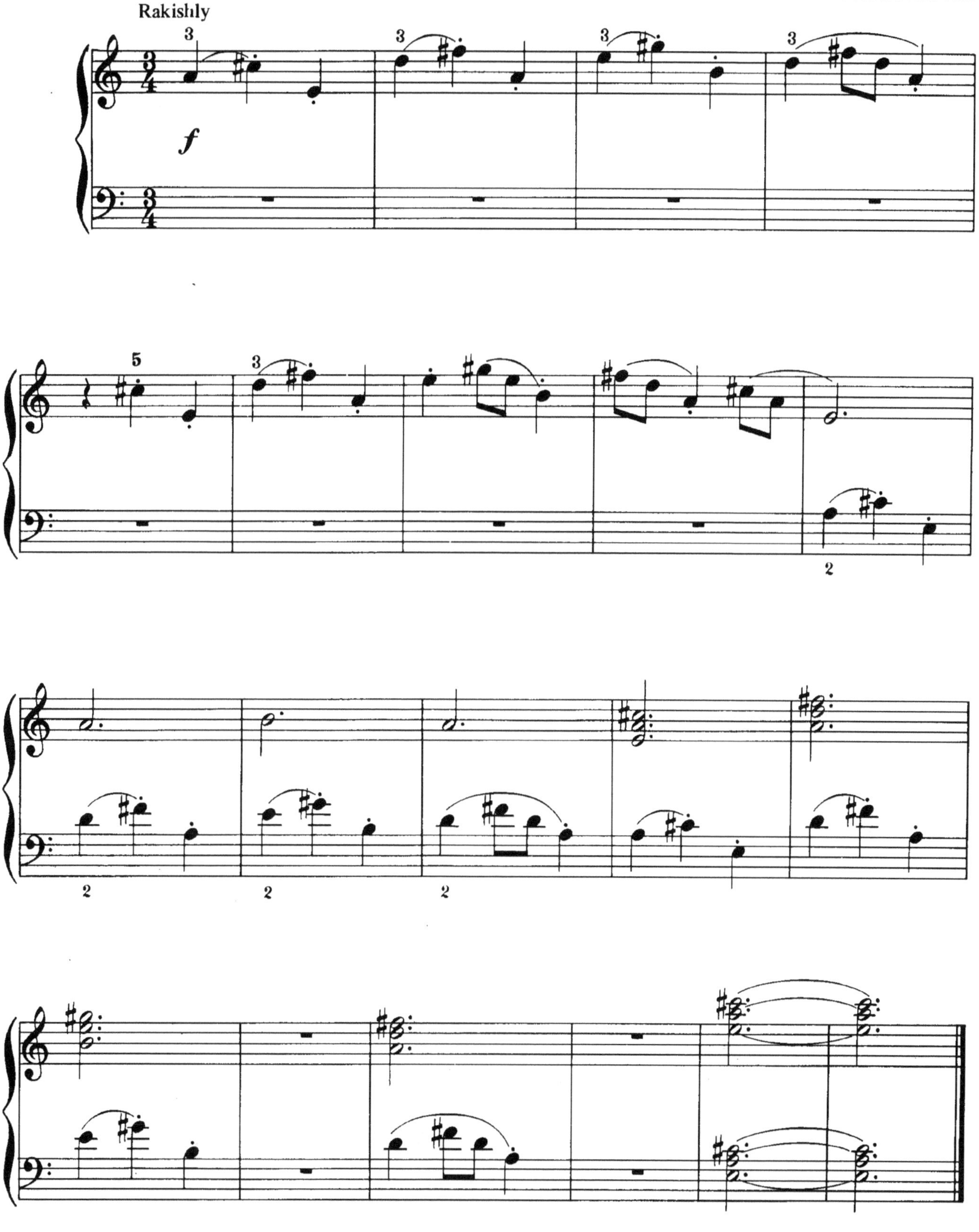

Triads (2nd Inversion): A—D—E; Ab—Db—Eb Major

PROCESSIONAL

Grandly

PAUL SHEFTEL

ECHOS

PAUL SHEFTEL

SUMMARY OF SECTIONS

MAJOR SCALES

The major scales can be divided into three groups. The scales within a group use the same fingering.

GROUP I: 0 to 4 sharps (C, G, D, A and E)—page 2

R.H.—4th finger on 7th step

L.H.—4th finger on 2nd step

GROUP II: 1 to 4 flats (F, B♭, E♭, and A♭)—page 17

R.H.—4th finger on B♭ (Exception: F scale ends on 4.)

L.H.—4th finger on 4th step (Exception: F scale is fingered like Group I scales.)

GROUP III: the enharmonic scales having 5 to 7 sharps or flats (B/C♭, F♯/G♭, C♯/D♭) —page 33

The fingering is parallel: both hands use fingers 2 and 3 on the two black keys and 2, 3, and 4 on the three. Thumbs fall on the white keys between the black key groups.

INTERVALS

Intervals can also conveniently be studied in three groups:

GROUP I: perfect 4ths and 5ths—page 8

GROUP II: major 2nds, 3rds, 6ths and 7ths—page 22

GROUP III: minor 2nds, 3rds, 6ths, 7ths and tritones—page 37

There is no unifying principle for the intervals within a group with the exception of Group I (always white to white or black to black except when the interval contains an F and a B). Each interval, however, has its own specific black-white pattern. These patterns are illustrated in the text.

MAJOR TRIADS—pages 11, 28, 43

The major triads can also be thought of in three groups. Each group has the same pattern of white and black keys.

GROUP I: C, F and G (all white)   G♭ (all black)

GROUP II: A, D and E (1 black)   A♭, D♭ and E♭ (1 white)

GROUP III: B (2 blacks)   B♭ (2 whites)

www.ingramcontent.com/pod-product-compliance
Lightning Source LLC
LaVergne TN
LVHW081322060426
835509LV00015B/1637